Life of Fred®

Cats

Life of Fred®
Cats

Stanley F. Schmidt, Ph.D.

Polka Dot Publishing

ISBN: 978-0-9791072-6-9

Library of Congress Catalog Number: 2011924326
Printed and bound in the United States of America

Polka Dot Publishing   Reno, Nevada

To order copies of books in the Life of Fred series,

visit our website PolkaDotPublishing.com

Questions or comments? Email the author at lifeoffred@yahoo.com

Ninth printing

Life of Fred: Cats was illustrated by the author with additional clip art furnished under license from Nova Development Corporation, which holds the copyright to that art.

for Goodness' sake

or as J.S. Bach—who was
never noted for his plain
English—often expressed it:

Ad Majorem Dei Gloriam
(to the greater glory of God)

If you happen to spot an error that the author, the publisher, and the printer missed, please let us know with an email to: lifeoffred@yahoo.com .

As a reward, we'll email back to you a list of all the corrections that readers have reported.

A Note Before We Begin

Bedtime reading? Each chapter is six pages—a perfect length. Or a first-thing-after-breakfast reading. Or a right-after-lunch activity.

A chapter each day will be something to look forward to.

At the end of each chapter is a Your Turn to Play.

Have a paper and pencil handy before you sit down to read.

Each Your Turn to Play consists of about three or four questions. They are not the boring workbook sheets that many elementary math books have: a million problems that are all alike.

Instead, the Your Turn to Play questions are fun. And some of them actually require . . . thought!

Have your child write out the answers—not just orally answer them.

After *all* the questions are answered, then take a peek at my answers that are given on the next page. At this point your child has *earned* the right to go on to the next chapter.

Don't allow your child to just read the questions and look at the answers. Your child won't learn as much taking that shortcut.

WHAT WE WANT FOR OUR KIDS

We have high aspirations for them. They will climb peaks, see things, and experience joys.

Today, the world is changing so fast that predicting what it will look like on their 21st birthday is almost impossible.

Many of us can't even name the little electronic "thingys" that kids are carrying around and playing with today.

The only safe prediction is that the world will be different.

Fred and I would like to join you for a while as we walk into that future.

Here are my bets as to what will be crucial
for your child's education . . .

1. **Reading** will be increasingly important.

When your child was five years old, almost everything he or she learned was what someone told him or her.

In college, half of what is learned is from reading.

In a graduate school history class, you don't watch WWII movies; you read about it.

Most of those who really excel in business, in the clergy, in science, or engineering—read and read and read.

The *Life of Fred* series encourages reading as no other math curriculum does. Many moms have reported that their kids want to do more than one lesson a day.

2. Learning how the mathematics **fits into real life** is critical.

Every math teacher is asked, "When are we ever gonna use this stuff?"

In Fred's life, he *first* encounters the need for some piece of math, and *then* we do it—everything from patterns of hearts drawn in the snow

smooth   fluffy   smooth fluffy   smooth   fluffy   smooth

(which we do in Chapter 4) to hyperbolic trig functions (in *Life of Fred: Calculus*).

3. Your child's education should be **integrated**.

Does it make sense to place the subjects into little watertight compartments? Are there no connections between science and history? Are there no connections between art, music, and mathematics?

This book does teach $7 + 6 = 13$ and that the cardinality of the set $\{\odot, \text{✈}, \text{☎}\}$ is 3, and a zillion other pieces of mathematics.[*]

But . . . be advised . . . I teach children—not mathematics. An integrated education, where all the parts of life flow together, is paramount in my thought.

In this book, your kids (and you!) see broad vistas:

✓ Astronomy. The Big Dipper is not a constellation. (Chapter 1)

✓ Human relations. The loudest talker is sometimes the least important person. (Chapter 2)

✓ Physiology. Why the clerk at C. C. Coalback's Electric Heater store looks so tired.

✓ Music. The full piano score for Fred's song "Happy." (Chapter 5)

✓ Geography. The four major oceans of the world. (Chapter 13)

✓ English. Fred's collection of homonyms. (Chapter 14)

. . . and oil painting, how Magellan named the Pacific Ocean, and four-dimensional cubes.

---

[*] The *Life of Fred* series contains **more mathematics** than any other math curriculum that I know of.

Contents

Chapter One
The Big Dipper

Fred's eyes went open. He was cold. He hugged his doll Kingie close to him. He still felt cold.

With his flashlight, he looked at the clock on the wall of his office. It was 2 a.m.—two hours after midnight.

He got out of his sleeping bag and walked over to turn on the lights.

With the light on, he could see his footprints in the frost on the floor. Fred knew that it was cold outside. It was a February Tuesday in Kansas.

Something was wrong.

Did I leave the window open? he thought to himself. He checked. The window was closed.

Last night when Fred went to bed he could see Orion through the window.

Now when he looked through the window, he saw a different constellation.

Big Flea?

This official constellation is called Ursa Major (Big Bear). Most of the stars in Ursa Major are hard to see.

But there are seven stars in Ursa Major that lots of people recognize. They form the Big Dipper. In fact, those seven stars are so famous that they are on the Alaska state flag.

State Flag of Alaska

A dipper is like a ladle.

ladle

If you are ever lost at night, the Big Dipper can help you find your way. The two stars at the end of the dipper point to the North Star. The North Star is north.

How to find the North Star

Fred shivered. He put on a shirt and pants over his pajamas.

He put on his socks and his shoes. He giggled and thought to himself: *Putting on shoes and socks are not* **commutative**. It does make a difference which order you do them. Putting on socks and then shoes gives you a different result than putting on shoes and then socks.

Addition is commutative. If you add 3 + 6 you get 9. If you add 6 + 3 you will also get 9.

Subtraction is not commutative. Nine take away three (9 − 3) makes sense. If you have nine cows and you take away three of them, you will have six cows left.

$$9 - 3 = 6$$

On the other hand, what does 3 − 9 mean? If you start with three cows, it is really hard to take away nine cows. It would be like putting on your shoes before putting on your socks.

            $3 - 9 = ?$

Fred opened his office door and headed out into the hallway. (Definitely not commutative. He would have had real difficulty getting into the hallway and then opening the door.)

The nine vending machines were humming quietly. Five on one side and four on the other. The hallway was as cold as his office.

Fred skipped the ice-cold Sluice machine. He ignored the Icy Ice Cream machine.

Instead, he chose the hot chocolate. For forty cents you get hot chocolate and a mug.

He took some nickels out of his pocket and counted out 40¢.

He carried the mug of hot chocolate back to his office and put it right next to Kingie. He knew that a cup of hot chocolate would keep his doll warm. Fred, himself, wasn't very hungry or thirsty right now.

Please take out a piece of paper and write your answers down before checking your work on the next page. Please.

Your Turn to Play

1. Are brushing your teeth and combing your hair commutative?

2. The Big Dipper has four stars in the cup and three stars in the handle. How many stars are in the Big Dipper?

$$4 + 3 = ?$$

3. The Big Dipper is not an official constellation. (Many adults do not know that.) The Big Dipper is an asterism—a pattern of stars that is not an official constellation.

Orion's belt is an asterism.

There are five vowels in English: A, E, I, O, and U.

This is the set of vowels in the word *asterism*: {a, e, i}. What is the cardinal number associated with this set?

. . . . **ANSWERS** . . . .

1. It doesn't matter whether you brush your teeth first or comb your hair first. These two things are commutative.

2. $4 + 3 = 7$

Four stars plus three stars equals seven stars.

In algebra, you will do the same thing with letters:

$$4x + 3x = 7x$$
$$4y + 3y = 7y$$
$$4abc + 3abc = 7abc$$

3. The cardinal number associated with {a, e, i} is 3. The cardinality of a set is the number of members in the set. (We did this in Chapter 16 of the previous book: *Life of Fred: Butterflies*.)

The cardinality of {#, $, @, ✂, ✈} is 5.

The cardinality of { } is 0.

Chapter Two
Talking with Sam

Even the doorknob felt cold. Fred went back out into the hallway. The only other person in the building was Sam, the janitor. He had his office at the end of the hallway.

Like his brothers, Nedrick, Ralph, and Lawrence, he had a big flashing, neon sign.

SAMUEL P. WISTROM

MATH DEPARTMENT BUILDING

CHIEF INSPECTOR/PLANNER/REMEDIATOR

FOR OFFICES 225-324

In contrast to Sam's flashing sign was the piece of paper that Fred had put on his door:

Fred Gauss
—room 314—

8–9 Arithmetic
9–10 Beginning Algebra
10–11 Advanced Algebra
11–noon Geometry   ⟵ - - - - - - - - - Small print.
noon–1 Trigonometry   Not flashing.
1–2 Calculus
2–3 Statistics
3–3:05 Break
3:05–4 Linear Algebra
4–5 Seminar in Biology, Economics,
        Physics, Set Theory, Topology, and Metamathematics.

⇨ The one with the biggest sign

    ⇨ the loudest talker

       ⇨ the one with the most titles

is sometimes the least important person.

Fred knocked on Sam's door. He could hear the television playing inside.

When Sam came to the door, he had a bowl of candy in his hand. He said, "Hi, Fred. What's up?"

Fred could feel the heat pouring out of Sam's office.

Sam said, "Come on in boy. I don't want to let all the heat out."

Fred went in and Sam closed the door. The TV was so loud that Fred had to shout: "What's wrong with the heat in the building? It's as cold in the hallway and in my office as it is outside."

Sam handed Fred the campus newspaper.

THE KITTEN Caboodle

The Official Campus Newspaper of KITTENS University   Tuesday 1 a.m.   10¢

University Orders Freeze

KANSAS: This morning the KITTENS University president ordered a hiring freeze. He had read that other universities were having a hiring freeze, so he wanted one too.

University president declares that KITTENS will not be left behind in the Freeze Race

Sam told Fred, "The president has ordered a freeze. I'm doing my part. I turned off the heat in the building."

Fred tried to explain to Sam that a *hiring freeze* has nothing to do with temperature. A hiring freeze means that the university is not employing new people right now.

Sam didn't understand. He pointed to the headline, "University Orders Freeze," and told Fred that those were his orders. (Sam only read headlines and never the articles.)

He noticed that Sam had an electric space heater that was keeping his office warm.

Sam offered Fred some candy. Fred said he wasn't hungry right now. He thanked Sam and headed out into the hallway.

2:15 a.m.

For a moment, Fred wasn't certain what he would do. It was a quarter after two in the morning, and he couldn't just go back to bed and freeze.

small essay

What Does a Quarter Mean?

When you divide something into four equal pieces, you get a quarter.

If you divide a pie into four equal pieces, each piece is a quarter of the pie.

If you divide an hour into four equal pieces, each piece is a quarter of an hour.

Sometimes a quarter is written as $\frac{1}{4}$. This is one part out of four.

end of small essay

Fred thought of putting on a lot of clothes so that he could stay warm.

Two hats
Six shirts
Four pants
Three pair of socks
Rubber boots

He thought of asking Sam if he could stay in his warm office for the night. Then he remembered Sam's loud television. Fred would never get to sleep.

He thought of going over to Alexander's apartment. His student, Alexander, would certainly let him stay there. It would be warm, and he could sleep on Alexander's couch. But it was 2:15 in the morning, and he didn't want to wake Alexander up.

Your Turn to Play

1. Silly question: What do you call the coin that is worth one-quarter of a dollar?

2. $2 + 5 = ?$

3. Are going into your bathroom and brushing your teeth commutative?

4. Is 15 minutes after 8 the same thing as a quarter after 8?

5. $9 - 7 = ?$

6. The number twenty-six written in numerals is 26. What is one thousand written as numerals?

.......ANSWERS.......

1. If we take a dollar and divide it into four equal parts, we get four quarters.

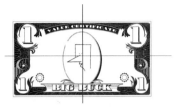

$1 = 100¢ = 25¢ + 25¢ + 25¢ + 25¢

25¢ =    It is called a quarter.

2. 2 + 5 = 7

3. No, they are not commutative. Most people keep their toothbrushes in the bathroom. It would be very hard to first brush your teeth and then head into the bathroom.

4. 8:15 = 15 minutes after 8
        = a quarter after 8

        Yes.

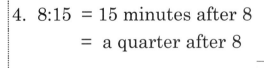

5. 9 − 7 = 2   (since 2 + 7 = 9)

6. One thousand written as numerals is 1,000.

Chapter Three
Open 24 Hours

There was one obvious thing that Fred could do. He could buy an electric space heater like the one that Sam has.

He ran back to his office and looked in the phone book.

Ashley's Electric Heaters—Stay warm! Open 9–5
Chris's Electric Heaters—None finer! Open 9–5
C. C. Coalback's Heaters—Buy one now! Open 24 hours
Dale's Electric Heaters—An honest deal with Dale! Open 9–5

It looked like Fred had only one choice. Only one of the four stores was open at 2:15 a.m.

He took a bag of nickels that was in his desk and headed out the door,
down the hallway,
down the stairs, and
out into the cold night.

Fred ran to keep warm. C. C. Coalback's store was about three blocks away.

C. C. Coalback Electric Heaters
We never close!

Fred was so happy that a store was open at this time in the morning.

The clerk in the store didn't seem to be as happy.

"Hey kid," she said. "What do you want?"

This seemed like a strange question to Fred. He was in a store that sold electric heaters, and he wanted to buy one. He noticed that she seemed very tired.

He shrugged his shoulders, held out his bag of nickels, and said, "I'd like to buy an electric space heater."

"How much money do you got?" she asked.

Fred emptied the bag of nickels onto the counter and began to count: 5, 10, 15, 20, 25, 30, 35, 40, 45, 50, 55, 60, 65, 70, 75, 80, 85, 90, 95, 100. He told her, "I have 100 cents, which is one dollar."

"Is that all you got?" she asked.

"I also have a twenty-dollar bill," he said as he took it out of his pocket to show her.

"That will do just fine. Twenty-one dollars will buy you a very nice heater." She took the nickels off the counter and took his $20 bill and headed into the back room of the store.

She took a heater that had a price tag of $5 on it.

She erased the $5.

She wrote $21 on the tag,

and brought the heater out to Fred.

She put it into a paper bag and handed it to Fred. This heater was in much poorer condition than the one that Sam had.*   Its electric cord was broken, and the heater was all banged up.

---

*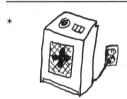

Fred was very trusting. He would never think of cheating anyone and didn't expect anyone would cheat him.

He ran back to the math building. He couldn't climb the stairs two-at-a-time like some older people do:

2   4   6   8   10   12   14   16   18

but he dreamed that if he ever got really tall, he would climb them three-at-a-time. He had never seen anyone do that.

3   6   9   12   15   18

He headed down the hallway—with 5 vending machines on one side and 4 on the other. Then quietly he opened his office door so that he wouldn't disturb Kingie.

The light was on in his office. It was 30 minutes after two in the morning, and Kingie was awake.

2:30

He told Fred that he had awoken and Fred wasn't there next to him. He had turned on the light and Fred wasn't anywhere in the office.

Kingie said, "I also was really cold and put on some extra clothes to stay warm until you got back."

Fred had only thought of putting on lots of clothes. Kingie had actually done it.

The scarf was a nice touch, but what really looked silly were the black boots. Kingie is a doll with a beanbag body. He doesn't have any feet.

Your Turn to Play

1. In the hallway there are five vending machines on one side and four on the other. How many vending machines are in the hallway?

2. Fred had given the clerk at C. C. Coalback's a dollar in nickels and a twenty-dollar bill.

$$\$1 + \$20 \ = \ ?$$

3. If the C. C. Coalback Electric Heater store is open 24 hours each day, how many hours is it closed each day?

4. C. C. Coalback is not a nice man. Instead of hiring three clerks who would each work 8 hours $(8 + 8 + 8 = 24)$, he just hired one clerk—his sister.

Why did she look so tired?

. . . . ANSWERS . . . .

1. $5 + 4 = 9$

Five vending machines plus four vending machines equals nine vending machines.

In algebra, we will do:

$$5v + 4v = 9v$$
$$5\sqrt{7x} + 4\sqrt{7x} = 9\sqrt{7x}$$
$$5\xi + 4\xi = 9\xi$$

The letter ξ is my favorite letter in the Greek alphabet. It is pronounced xi which rhymes with *eye*.

There are only 24 letters in the Greek alphabet. There are 26 letters in our alphabet.

We have two more letters than they do. $26 - 24 = 2$

2. $\$1 + \$20 = \$21$

3. Since there are 24 hours in a day and the store is open 24 hours each day, it never closes. $24 - 24 = 0$

It is closed zero hours each day.

4. If Coalback's sister is the only one working in a store that never closes, she will get really, really, really, really, really, really, really, really, really, really, really, really sleepy.

Chapter Four
Hoodwinked

red told Kingie that he didn't have to worry about getting warm. He had bought a brand new electric heater that would make his office toasty warm.

He took it out of the paper bag and showed it to Kingie.

Kingie kept all his clothes on.

When Fred went to plug it in, he noticed that the wire was broken and the plug was missing.

missing

He saw that the heater was dented and there were rust spots on it.

"The clerk must have made a mistake," Fred said to Kingie. "She must have accidentally given me a heater that they were going to throw away. I'll take it back and get it exchanged for the right one."

Kingie kept all his clothes on.

Fred headed out of his office, down the hallway past the nine vending machines (5 on one side and 4 on the other), down the stairs, and out into the cold night.

He ran the three blocks to keep warm.
When he got to the store, a little surprise
awaited him.

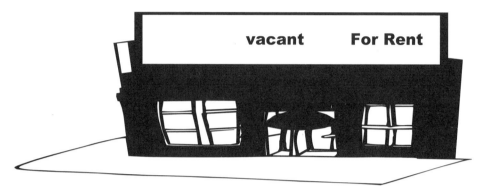

Fred began to realize
. . . that he had been deceived,
  . . . that he had been cheated,
        hoodwinked,
        tricked,
        bamboozled,
        defrauded, and
        victimized.
In short, Fred had been taken in.

A little tear came to his eye. It wasn't a big
tear, just a little one. He was cold and didn't
like losing $21. But he was also saddened by
the thought of C. C. Coalback and his sister. He
was sad that there were people who decide to
cheat and lie. Fred didn't hate them. He was
sorry for them.

On the way back to his office, he found a KITTENS public trash can.

There were a couple of inches of snow on the ground. As Fred walked, he spotted a heart that someone had drawn in the snow.

How nice, Fred thought. *It's February and Valentine's Day is coming up. I bet someone is thinking of his sweetheart.*

Then Fred saw a second heart drawn in the snow. This one artistic and fluffy.

Then he saw a ♡ and another ♡.

As he looked down the sidewalk they seemed to form a pattern:

smooth   fluffy   smooth fluffy   smooth   fluffy   smooth

Fred is a mathematician, and one of the fun things that mathematicians love to do is find patterns. Fred predicted that the next heart would be a fluffy one.

And he was right.

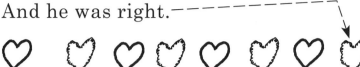

smooth   fluffy   smooth fluffy   smooth   fluffy   smooth   fluffy

He thought of smooth as S and fluffy as F:
S F S F S F S F. . . .

On the next street, someone had drawn a different pattern:

Now it was Smooth hearts and Broken hearts: S S B S S B S S B. . . .
What would be next?

He looked for a pattern. The hearts seemed to come in groups of three:
　　　　S S B   S S B   S S B. . . .
That made it easy to guess what was coming next:

　　S S B　　　S S B　　　S S B　　　S. . . .

Your Turn to Play

1. Some patterns are super easy to see. What is the next one going to be?

fluffy   fluffy   fluffy   fluffy   fluffy   fluffy   fluffy

2. How many are a dozen? (This is from the previous book.)

3. 3 + 4 = ?

4. What is the next one in this sequence?

fluffy   broken   fluffy   broken   fluffy   broken   fluffy

5. Example: In numerals it would be 100. In words it is one hundred.

 Your turn: In numerals it would be 1,000. What would it be in words?

6. Fred noticed that the trees that had been planted along the sidewalk were in a pattern.

deciduous   deciduous   evergreen   deciduous   deciduous   evergreen   deciduous   deciduous   evergreen

 What will the next tree be?

·······ANSWERS·······

1. A good guess would be

   fluffy

2. A dozen is 12.

3. 3 + 4 = 7

4. The next one will be

   fluffy   broken   fluffy   broken   fluffy   broken   fluffy   broken

5. In words, 1,000 is one thousand.

6. If we start with . . .

   deciduous   deciduous   evergreen   deciduous   deciduous   evergreen   deciduous   deciduous evergreen

   D   D   E   D   D   E   D   D   E

this could be written as   DDE DDE DDE and now
it's easy to see that the next tree will be D. Deciduous.

(Deciduous means that it loses its leaves in winter.)

Chapter Five
Found

F red was happy. Losing $21 or being cold didn't keep him from being grateful for everything that God had given him. And being thankful is the secret to happiness.

As he walked back to the math building, he made up a little song to sing.

It's easy to see a pattern in his song. All the measures are alike. It was like the pattern

fluffy

fluffy

fluffy

Fred wasn't very good at composing songs.

He wasn't very good at art.

His five-year-old voice was high and squeaky.

But he was very good at being thankful.

He was also good at math. As he walked along the street where they were doing construction, he thought he saw a pattern:

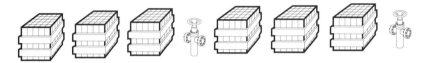

He was expecting the next thing to be

Fred was wrong. Instead it was

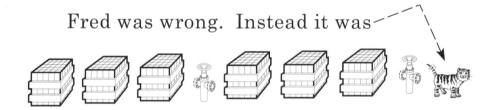

It was an unhappy cat shivering in the snow. It looked up at Fred and said, "Meow" in the saddest tones.

Fred picked her up. He wished that he had a scarf to wrap her up in, but Kingie was back at Fred's office using his scarf.

He carried her in his little bony five-year-old arms back to the math building. He wished he had arms like his twenty-year-old student Alexander. Alexander had big muscles, and that would keep the kitten warmer than Fred's bony arms.

 The kitten looked up at Fred and made kitten noises:

Meow, purr, purr, purr, meow, purr, purr, purr, meow, purr, purr, purr.

Fred recognized the pattern in MPPP MPPP MPPP.

Fred thought he understood what the kitten was saying to him. *Meow* must have meant "Daddy," and *purr purr purr* must have meant "I am hungry."

They entered the math building, and Fred carried the kitten up the two flights of stairs, down the hallway, and into his office.

"Look at the cute little kitten I found," Fred announced to Kingie. "She was saying to me, 'Daddy, I am hungry.' Don't you think she is soooo cute?"

Kingie had a little different reaction than Fred.

Which of these four basic emotions was Kingie feeling?

     ☐ Glad
     ☐ Sad
     ☐ Mad
     ☒ Afraid

Kingie knew something that Fred didn't know. Unfortunately, Fred wasn't looking at his doll (or listening to him). All Fred was doing was singing to his kitty:

Kitty Song

Did we mention that Fred wasn't very good at composing songs?

The kitten sang along with Fred: "Purr, purr, purr." Then Fred remembered that purr, purr, purr = I am hungry.*

"Kitty, do you want to stay here with my doll Kingie while I go down the hallway to get you something to eat from the vending machines?"

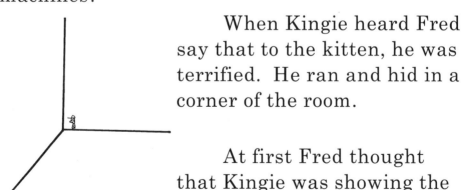

When Kingie heard Fred say that to the kitten, he was terrified. He ran and hid in a corner of the room.

At first Fred thought that Kingie was showing the

---

* *Purr, purr, purr* really doesn't mean "I am hungry." That is just what Fred thought it meant. As everyone knows, only people like Mary Poppins can understand what animals are really saying.

kitten how the edges of the room are orthogonal (meet at right angles). Fred knew that it is never too early to learn a little basic math. And almost everyone needs to know about right angles.

right angle   not a right angle   not a right angle

Your Turn to Play

1. If you sew, you have to know what right angles are. Suppose you are going to sew a pillowcase and you don't know about right angles. It might look like this:

On your paper, draw a pillowcase that has right angles.

2. Suppose you are an architect (a person who designs buildings). If you don't know about right angles, your building might look like this:

On your paper, draw a building with right angles.

3. 2 + 5 = ?

4. 7 + 2 = ?

5. How many is a dozen plus one?

6. What is the next one in this sequence:

·······ANSWERS·······

1. Here is my drawing of a pillowcase with right angles. Your drawing may be different.

2. Here is my drawing of a building with right angles.

3. 2 + 5 = 7

You can also write this as

$$\begin{array}{r} 2 \\ +\ 5 \\ \hline 7 \end{array}$$

4.
$$\begin{array}{r} 7 \\ +\ 2 \\ \hline 9 \end{array}$$

5. A dozen plus one is
$$\begin{array}{r} 12 \\ +\ 1 \\ \hline 13 \end{array}$$

6. ♩♩♩♩♩♩♩♩♩ can be seen as ♩♩♩♩ ♩♩♩♩ ♩♩

The next note will be ♩♩♩♩♩♩♩♩♩♩

Small Music Lesson

This is a quarter note: ♩   This is a half note: ♩

Chapter Six
Alone with the Cat

B ut Kingie wasn't talking about right angles when he was hiding in the corner of the room. He was screaming.

No! No! Don't leave me alone in the room with that cat!

Fred asked, "Why are you frightened? You and this cute little kitty could play together while I go down the hall to get something for her to eat."

When Fred said the word *eat*, Kingie started to climb the wall.

"Do you know what I look like?" Kingie shouted to Fred.

Fred shook his head.

"I look like, I look like, I look like . . ." Kingie couldn't finish his sentence. He pointed to the newspaper on Fred's desk.

THE KITTEN Caboodle

The Official Campus Newspaper of KITTENS University   Tuesday 2 a.m.   10¢

news update

Hiring Freeze Ends

KANSAS: This morning the KITTENS University president changed his mind. There will not be a hiring freeze.

University president found some money in a desk drawer.

advertisement

CAT TOYS!

"Oh good!" said Fred. "Sam will probably turn on the heat now."

Kingie said, "Look at the ad. Do you see that? Four of those cat toys look just like me."

"Oh," said Fred. He finally understood why Kingie was frightened. He told Kingie, "I'll take the kitty with me."

Fred and the kitty headed down the hall to look at the vending machines. Kingie shut the door as they left.

Fred walked down the hallway. The kitty was right beside him. They got to the vending machines—five on the right and four on the left. Fred thought:

$$5 \atop {+\,4} \over 9$$

"What would you like?" Fred asked his kitty. "There are doughnuts, ice cream, Sluice, candy bars, gum, pretzels. . . ."

Suddenly the kitty ran around to the back of one of the machines. There was a tiny squeak. The kitty came back with her breakfast in her mouth.

It was a little mouse.

Fred got a little sick looking at that. The kitty seemed very happy.

What he didn't understand was that cats are carnivores—meat eaters. If Fred had offered his kitty doughnuts, ice cream, Sluice, candy bars, gum, or pretzels from the vending machines, the kitty would not be interested at all. (Dogs might be. They have a much different digestive system than cats.)

Cats are more than just carnivores. They are **obligate carnivores**. Cats want meat for breakfast, meat for lunch, and meat for dinner.

Not just protein—they need animal protein.
Carnivores are animals that eat meat—for
example, dogs, cats, bears, seals, and weasels.

Obligate (pronounced OB-leh-git)
carnivores have no choice. They must eat meat.

Time Out!
English lesson

Adjectives are words that describe:
red hair, *tasty* pizza, *scared* Kingie,
and *obligate* carnivores.
Verbs are words that do things:
comb hair, *eat* pizza, *or hug* Kingie.

Because cats are obligate
carnivores they are obligated to eat
only meat.

Dogs and people can get all the protein
they need from plant combinations such as
beans and rice. Dogs and people ≠ cats.*

Some pet food companies put corn, wheat,
rice, and other carbohydrate fillers in their pet
food. But cats have no need for carbohydrates.

---

* The symbol ≠ means "not equal." For example, 2 + 2 = 4, but 2 + 2 ≠ 5.

Why do they put them in? Easy answer: Because corn, wheat, and rice are much cheaper than meat.

Which can is cheaper to make?

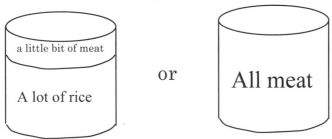

a little bit of meat

A lot of rice

or

All meat

Your Turn to Play

1. Copy these on a piece of paper and answer them:

5	3	8	2	6
+ 4	+ 6	+ 0	+ 7	+ 1

2. Bears will eat fish, pancakes, honey, peanut butter-and-jelly sandwiches, and doughnuts. Bears are carnivores, but are they obligate carnivores?

3. There are nine mice in the house. A cat eats two of them. How many are left in the house?   9
                                    − 2

4. What time is it?

· · · · · · · ANSWERS · · · · · · ·

1.

5	3	8	2	6
+ 4	+ 6	+ 0	+ 7	+ 1
9	9	8	9	7

2. Bears don't eat just meat. Pancakes, honey, peanut-butter-and-jelly sandwiches, and doughnuts have a lot of carbohydrates in them—and bears can easily digest them. Bears are not obligate carnivores.

3.
$$\begin{array}{r} 9 \\ -\ 2 \\ \hline 7 \end{array}$$

4. It is 2:40.

Sometimes people say that it is twenty minutes to three.

Today, we add four new facts: the numbers that add to 11.

Four facts to learn.

2	3	4	5
+ 9	+ 8	+ 7	+ 6
11	11	11	11

Please memorize them now, and they will be yours for the rest of your life.

Chapter Seven
Kingie's Fort

Fred noticed that his office door was closed. He thought he had left it open. When he tried to open it, he found that it was locked.

Kingie had shut the door and locked it.

Fred knocked on the door and said, "Open up Kingie. It's me."

Behind the closed door Kingie asked, "Is it just you?"

Fred answered, "I guess I should have said that it is us—me, the cat, and a dead mouse."

"Wait a minute," said Kingie. "Count to a hundred and then you can come in."

5, 10, 15, 20, 25, 30, 35, 40, 45, 50, 55, 60, 65, 70, 75, 80, 85, 90, 95, 100

It would have been even quicker if Fred had counted by tens: 10, 20, 30, 40, 50, 60, 70, 80, 90, 100.

Fred heard a click as the door was unlocked. He carefully opened the door. He looked inside the room. Kingie was nowhere to be seen.

What Fred did see was a little building in the corner of the room. It was about one foot tall.

I'll come out when the cat is gone!

Kingie had built this little fort when Fred and the cat were in the hallway.

With Kingie tucked away safely in his fort, Fred had a chance to look at his cat.

This is nature's killing machine.

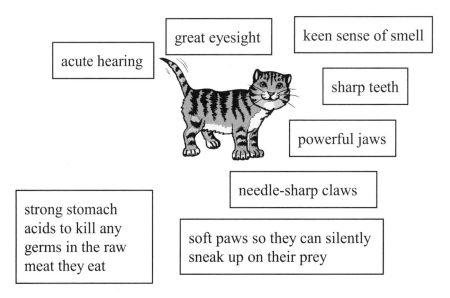

great eyesight

keen sense of smell

acute hearing

sharp teeth

powerful jaws

needle-sharp claws

strong stomach acids to kill any germs in the raw meat they eat

soft paws so they can silently sneak up on their prey

Fred was getting a bit sleepy. He had been up since 2 a.m.  He could feel the heat going on in the building. It was now 2:45, which some people call a quarter to three.

2:45 a.m.

Fred snuggled down into his sleeping bag under his desk. Fred was hoping to get a little sleep before dawn.

It felt nice to have the heat on in the building. Sam must have read the newspaper. Every minute the temperature was rising by two degrees:

36° 38° 40° 42° 44° 46° 48° 50° 52°

If Fred's new pet had been a puppy instead of a kitten, he would have lain down next to Fred, and the two of them would have slept.

But cats are different. They are born to hunt. From the moment that a kitten can walk, it will start training to be a hunter.

✓ It will start to explore. Using its great hearing, eyesight, and sense of smell, it looks in every corner of the room.

✓ It will sneak up on anything that is moving. Here is where the soft paws are helpful.

✓ It will pounce and attack anything that is moving, even its mother's tail. The sharp claws make it easy to hold onto anything it catches.

So the kitten went over to Kingie's fort. She could smell Kingie inside. She heard him moving. She tried to open the door to the fort, but Kingie had locked it from the inside.

Then she spotted a big pointy thing sticking out of the sleeping bag.

Slowly, quietly, she sneaked up on the big pointy thing. Then she leaped up. With her needle-sharp claws she seized the big pointy thing.

Fred screamed. The kitten held on for a moment and then ran to the other side of the room.

Your Turn to Play

1. In numerals, one million is 1,000,000.
What is a dozen in numerals?

2. If the kitten followed the pattern:

sneak-sneak-pounce-claw-sneak-sneak-pounce-claw-sneak-sneak-pounce-claw-sneak-sneak-. . .

what would be the next thing she would be doing?

3. Copy these on a piece of paper and answer them:

$$
\begin{array}{ccccc}
2 & 6 & 0 & 4 & 8 \\
+\ 7 & +\ 5 & +\ 2 & +\ 7 & -\ 1 \\
\hline
\end{array}
$$

4. What time is it?

5. What is the cardinality of the set of stars in Orion's belt? (There is a picture of Orion's belt on page 17.)

6. Fred had gotten into his sleeping bag and then he fell asleep. Are these two things commutative?

......ANSWERS.......

1. A dozen in numerals is 12.

2. *sneak-sneak-pounce-claw-sneak-sneak-pounce-claw-sneak-sneak-pounce-claw-sneak-sneak-...*

might be written as SSPCSSPCSSPCSS....

Break it apart into groups of four and you get:

SSPC SSPC SSPC SS....

The next item in that sequence will be P (*pounce*).

3.

2	6	0	4	8
+ 7	+ 5	+ 2	+ 7	− 1
9	11	2	11	7

4. It is 2:50. Some people call this ten minutes to three.

5. The set has three stars in it. The cardinality of the set is 3.

Two, if you happen to remember that one of the "stars" is a nebula.

6. They are not commutative. Getting into your sleeping bag and then falling asleep is easy to do. Falling asleep and then getting into your sleeping bag is either hard or impossible.

Chapter Eight
Pacific

Fred sat up. Some people would say that when the kitten attacked Fred's nose, she was just being "playful." (Some people call military exercises in which soldiers practice killing and blowing up things war *games*.)

In the five years that Kingie had lived with Fred, his doll had never done this to Fred. Kingie was very pacific.*

The scratches on his nose were very red. They hurt.

Time Out!
Geography lesson

Pacific
Ocean

Atlantic
Ocean

The Pacific Ocean is the biggest ocean in the world. The deepest place in the whole world is in the Pacific Ocean in the Mariana Trench.

---

* Pacific = calm, peaceful.

The deepest point in the Mariana Trench is 35,797 feet down. That's almost seven miles down. (There are 5,280 feet in a mile.)

So why is it called the Pacific Ocean?

Time Out!
History lesson

About five hundred years ago a man named Ferdinand Magellan took a little boat trip.

He started out from Spain in September, 1519 with five small ships and 270 men.

Two years later (1521) one ship with 18 men made it back to Spain. They had gone all the way around the world. They were the first people to ever sail around the world.

Later, you will learn how to do this fancy subtraction:

270 men started the trip
− 18 men finished the trip
252 men did not return to Spain

One of the hardest parts of the trip was getting around the southern tip of South America.

It took them 38 days to sail around the rough and stormy southern tip. (That's more than a month.)

Magellan and three ships made it around the southern tip.

```
   5  ships started the trip
 − 3  ships made it around the tip
   2  ships didn't get that far
```

When he got to the ocean that is west of South America (on the left), it was calm and peaceful. So he named it the Pacific Ocean (since *pacific* means calm and peaceful).

And that's how the Pacific Ocean got its name.

Five minutes to 3

Fred didn't know what to do. His nose really hurt. It was almost 3 a.m. and in about five hours he would be teaching his eight o'clock class. All his students would be asking about his nose.

Fred was having to deal with two different things:

     1) the pain of his nose, and

     2) the embarrassment.

The embarrassment was easier to deal with. Fred thought he might wear a very big hat to class that would cover his nose.

Now Fred was down to one problem:

     1) the pain of his nose.

But that broke into two problems:

     1) the actual pain, and

     2) the possibility of infection.

That kitty had been walking around in the dirt when he found her. That kitty had caught a mouse with its claws. Those claws that scratched Fred's nose were probably loaded with germs.*

Your Turn to Play

1. Germs are so small that there might be a million germs in the scratches on Fred's nose. Write one million in numerals.

2. This is the set of ships that Magellan started his trip with: {Trinidad, Concepcion, San Antonio, Victoria, Santiago}. What is the cardinality of that set?

3. This is the set of ships that made it around the world and back to Spain: {Victoria}. What is the cardinal number associated with that set?

4. What is the set of Magellan's ships that did not make it back to Spain?

5. What is the cardinality of the set of Magellan's ships that did not make it back to Spain?

---

* *Germs* is a word that everyone understands. You wash your hands after you go to the bathroom to get rid of the germs on your hands.

Germs cause infection—things get red and swollen. Can you imagine Fred with a swollen nose? That is beyond imagining.

Fred liked to sound scientific. Instead of *germs*, he would often say *disease-causing bacteria.* Bacteria are super tiny things that you can only see with a microscope.

. . . . ANSWERS . . . .

1. One million in numerals is 1,000,000.

2. The cardinality of {Trinidad, Concepcion, San Antonio, Victoria, Santiago} is 5.

3. The cardinal number associated with {Victoria} is 1.

4. Victoria made it back to Spain. The set of ships that didn't make it back = {Trinidad, Concepcion, San Antonio, Santiago}.

5. The cardinality of {Trinidad, Concepcion, San Antonio, Santiago} is 4.

A Row of Practice

Cover the gray answers with a blank sheet of paper. Write your answers on your paper.

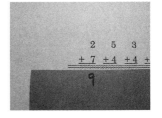

Then after you have done the whole row, check your answers.

2	5	3	2	4	7	6	12
+ 7	+ 4	+ 4	+ 9	+ 3	+ 2	+ 1	+ 1
9	9	7	11	7	9	7	13

Chapter Nine
When in Doubt—Read

The kitten was on the other side of the room licking her paws. Kingie was safe in his fort. Suddenly, Fred noticed that his sleeping bag had drops of blood on it.

Almost everyone gets nosebleeds where blood comes from the inside of the nose.

Fred was different. He had a bleeding nose.

He didn't know what to do. He got up and headed to his books that lined the walls of his office. It was easy to find the book he needed since he had put his books in alphabetical order.

Castanets for Everyday Use
Casual Pizza Restaurants
Cat Scratches: What to Do
Cattleman: What It Takes to Be One[*]

---

[*] *Cattleman: What It Takes to Be One* is a very short book. It has only one page, and there is only one word on that page.

Cattle

Fred selected:

Chapter One told Fred:

If you want to avoid bites, scratches and rabies[*] . . .

● Don't deal with strange animals that you meet on the street. (Fred failed that one.)

● Don't leave pet alone with a young child. (At age five, would Fred be considered young?)

● Select your family pet carefully. (Fred didn't do any careful selection.)

● Make sure your cat has her rabies shot. (Fred didn't do that.)

---

[*] RAY-bees Rabies is a disease that was known in 300 B.C., but it took until 1804 before they figured out how it was transmitted. It is transmitted from the saliva (spit) of a rabid animal. From 300 B.C. to 1804 is about 2100 years.

$$300 \text{ B.C.} \to\to\to\to\to\to 0 \to\to\to\to\to\to\to\to\to\to 1804$$

$$300 \quad + \quad 1804 \qquad\qquad \begin{array}{r} 300 \\ + 1804 \\ \hline 2104 \text{ years} \end{array}$$

Chapter Two of *Cat Scratches: What to Do* said . . .

If you picked up some stray cat or dog off the street and took it home and it bit or scratched you enough to break the skin, think about rabies.

If you don't know whether it has had its rabies shot, go to the doctor and take the animal with you.

Chapter Three . . .

Cat scratches and bites can often be deep. Wash the wound gently with warm running water for about five minutes. Use soap. Rinse well. Cat's claws contain bacteria (germs) that can give you Cat Scratch Fever.[*]

Chapter Four . . .

Cat scratches to the face (or hands) can cause scars. Getting to a doctor can help prevent that.

After reading Prof. Eldwood's book, Fred knew what to do. First, he headed down the hallway to the restroom and washed his wounds. They bled a lot, but that was much better than getting Cat Scratch Fever.

Then he headed back to his office. He told Kingie, "The kitty and I are heading off to the doctor at the campus hospital."

---

[*] Cat Scratch Fever is real. It is an infection that can give you serious problems.

From inside his fort, Kingie said, "That's fine with me."

Fred and the kitty headed down the hallway, down two flights of stairs, and out into the cold February air. It was a quarter after three.

3:15 a.m.

3:20

In five minutes they arrived at the hospital.

They made Fred fill out a form.

He returned the completed form to the receptionist and was told that it would be about an hour before he would see the doctor.

He looked at the magazines:

LOSE 20 POUNDS!

Fred didn't want to do that. He weighs 37 pounds. He didn't want to weigh 17 pounds.

$$\begin{array}{r} 37 \\ -\ 20 \\ \hline 17 \end{array}$$

WEDDING DRESSES FOR $3,000!

Fred wasn't interested.

Your Turn to Play

1. There were three other people in the waiting room. Is 3 a cardinal number or an ordinal number?

2. Fred was the fourth person. Is fourth a cardinal number or an ordinal number?

3. Fred was sitting on a sofa*. The cat made a vertical ($\updownarrow$) scratch in it. Then a horizontal($\leftrightarrow$) scratch. The pattern was: VHHHVHHHVHHHV. . . . What would be the direction of the next scratch?

4. Write a complete English sentence that would describe how the chesterfield would look after the kitty worked on it for an hour.

---

* Sofa = couch = chesterfield = divan.

· · · · · · · ANSWERS · · · · · · ·

1. Three is a cardinal number. The cardinal numbers are used to count the members of a set.

The cardinal number associated with {#, $} is 2.

The cardinal number associated with {✏, ✂, ☎} is 3.

The cardinal number associated with { } is 0.

2. Fourth is an ordinal number. The ordinal numbers are first, second, third, fourth, fifth, sixth. . . .

3. VHHHVHHHVHHHV . . . can be thought of as
   VHHH VHHH VHHH V. . . .

The next one in the sequence is H.

Either "H" or "horizontal" would be considered correct.

4. Your answer may be different than mine. Here are several of my answers:

   ☆ After an hour, the sofa would look terrible.

   ☆ The chesterfield would look like a mess.

   ☆ After the kitty worked on it for an hour, the divan would be ready to go to the dump.

   ☆ It would be worthless.

Sentences always start with a capital letter.

Sentences always end with a period (.) or an exclamation point (!) or a question mark (?).

Chapter Ten
At the Doctor's

An hour had passed. Fred had started waiting at 3:20 a.m., and it was now 4:20 a.m. The other three people in the waiting room had already been called in.

The kitty was taking a little nap next to the couch she had destroyed.

The nurse opened the door and called for Fred Goose. Fred said, "It's Gauss, not Goose. It sounds like *house*."

Fred got up and followed the nurse. The kitty woke up and followed Fred.

In the examination room, the nurse took Fred's temperature and then checked his blood pressure.

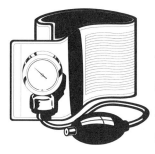

The blood pressure cuff was too big for Fred's little arm. He only weighs 37 pounds. She found a tiny one for small children and used it.

"The doctor will be with you shortly," she told Fred as she left the room.

It was 4:20 when Fred and the kitty entered the examination room. Fred's nose still hurt. The kitty passed the time playing with the blood pressure cuff. She pretended it was a mouse. She would

4:35 a.m.

pounce on it and then chew the rubber tube.

After 15 minutes, the doctor came in. He looked at Fred and exclaimed, "What happened to you?" Fred pointed to his kitty and then to his nose.

By now the blood pressure cuff had changed from ![] into ![] .

The doctor took one look at the cat and asked Fred, "Where did you get that?"

"She's my kitty," Fred explained. "I found her this morning after I had tried to return an electric heater which was no good since its electric plug was missing. I needed the heater because the building was cold since the janitor had turned off the heat, having misread the newspaper thinking that the headline of

'University Orders Freeze' meant that the heat should be turned off."

The doctor interrupted, "But where did you get the cat?" The doctor was experiencing what is called TMD.*

Fred continued, "And so I was walking back to my office when I noticed patterns in the snow." Fred took a piece of paper from the doctor's desk and wrote:

smooth   fluffy   smooth fluffy   smooth   fluffy   smooth

"WHERE DID YOU FIND THAT CAT!" the doctor shouted.

This was getting to be WTMD.**

"Oh," said Fred. "She was right after

and I was expecting a ⬚ and there was a kitty instead."

---

* TMD = Too Much Detail.

** WTMD = Way Too Much Detail

The doctor took Fred's arm and they headed out into the hallway. The doctor shut the door to the examination room. He said to Fred, "Do you realize . . ."

He showed him the newspaper.

THE KITTEN Caboodle

The Official Campus Newspaper of KITTENS University

Tuesday 3 a.m.   10¢

news flash

Tiger Cub Escapes

KANSAS: Early this morning the whole campus was put on alert. One of the four tiger cubs has escaped from the university zoo.

University president said that he didn't know anything about the missing tiger cub.

Mama missing one of her cubs

$$4$$
$$-\ 1$$
$$3 \text{ cubs left}$$

WARNING!

If you see the cub, do not approach it—danger!
Call the KITTENS University Zoo and specially trained men will come and capture it.

All Fred could say was, "Oops."
The doctor called the zoo.

Your Turn to Play

1. If the tiger had 7 cubs and 2 escaped, how many would be left?

2. A tiger cub has 5 claws on each foot.*

Counting by fives, how many would she have on all four feet?

3. Here are ten mice that would make a nice lunch for a tiger cub. Counting by twos, how many eyes do these ten mice have?

4. Write the set of the five vowels in English.
Here is a start: {A, . . .

5. The phone call to the zoo cost a quarter.
How many cents is that?

---

* As everyone knows who has been scratched by a cat, cats have 5 claws on their front feet and 4 on their back feet. Let's assume for this problem that they have 5 claws on each foot.

·······ANSWERS·······

1. A tiger had 7 cubs and 2 escaped.

$$\begin{array}{r} 7 \\ -\,2 \\ \hline 5 \end{array}$$

2.

    5 10 15 20

3.

    2   4   6   8   10   12   14   16   18   20

4. The set of vowels is {A, E, I, O, U}.

5. If we take a dollar and divide it into four equal parts, we get four quarters.

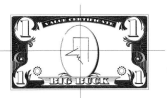

$1 = 100¢ = 25¢ + 25¢ + 25¢ + 25¢

 = 25¢

Chapter Eleven
Saying Goodbye

Fred didn't know what to do. He was standing in the hallway of the hospital while his kitty was inside the examination room. The doctor had gone down the hall to phone the zoo.

He went back into the examination room to say goodbye to his kitty.

In the room was the examination table where the patient could sit. It had been covered with a white sheet of paper. Kitty had shredded the paper into confetti.

She was having fun doing what cats do.

He figured that if he taught his kitty something, she would calm down. *What to teach my kitty?* Fred wondered.

He decided to teach her something about reading since he knew that she wasn't very good at reading.

He began: "Every word in English contains at least one vowel. The vowels are A, E, I, O, and U." Fred wrote those words on a piece of paper and showed them to his kitty.

He underlined all the vowels.

<u>Eve</u>ry w<u>o</u>rd <u>i</u>n <u>E</u>ngl<u>i</u>sh c<u>o</u>nt<u>ai</u>ns <u>a</u>t l<u>ea</u>st <u>o</u>ne v<u>o</u>w<u>e</u>l. Th<u>e</u> v<u>o</u>w<u>e</u>ls <u>a</u>re <u>A</u>, <u>E</u>, <u>I</u>, <u>O</u>, <u>a</u>nd <u>U</u>.

Kitty took the paper and chewed on it.

Fred invented a word game to show the kitty all the vowels. On another piece of paper he wrote *cat, cet, cit, cot, cut*. But cet and cit didn't make any sense.

He tried again: *May, me, might, mow, Mut*. Each word says its own vowel.

This time they all made sense:

May = fifth month of the year

me

might

mow

Mut = the German word for courage—rhymes
 with *flute*

Fred knew that kitties understand German as well as they understand English.

Fred found a children's book in the magazine rack.

He thought *Maybe reading her a story would be better. Some cats don't like to play word games.*

The kitty could see regular English words and the five vowels and learn that every word contains at least one vowel.

Prof. Eldwood's

Tales
for
Tiny Tots

Fred opened the book and began to read:

Why cry, my pygmy fly? Thy gypsy hymns ply the sky!*

a vowel!

The kitty started laughing.

---

* There is a very short list of English words that don't contain a vowel. Here are the 23 I could think of: *by, cry, dry, fly, fry, gypsy, hymn, lymph, lynch, Lynn, lynx, myth, my, ply, pygmy, rhythm, shy, sky, spry, thy, try, tryst,* and *why*. There are somewhere between a half million (500,000) and a million (1,000,000) words in the English language. The average person might use, say, 20,000 words in speaking.

Twenty-three words out of 20,000 are not very many.

There was a knock on the door. Two men from the KITTENS Zoo came in. They wore leather pants and shirts and long leather gloves. They had helmets with plastic face shields.

One of them had a net and a tranquilizer gun. The other had a cage.

Fred knew what to do. He went over and picked up his kitty. She licked his nose. He put her in the cage.

The men left without a word. They were in shock. They didn't expect the capture to be that easy.

The nurse came in and groaned when she saw the mess that the tiger cub had made. She threw all the shredded paper into the garbage and began to stack the pill boxes that were scattered all over the floor.

She put them in stacks of ten.

It was easy to see that there were 32 boxes.

tens	ones
3	2

Your Turn to Play

How many boxes?

1.

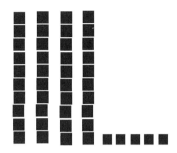

2.

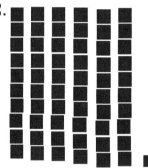

3.

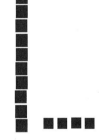

4. What is the next note in the sequence?

. . . . ANSWERS . . . .

tens ones

1.   4   5   forty-five

tens ones

2.   6   1   sixty-one

tens ones

3.   1   4   fourteen

4. ♩♩♩♩♩♩♩♩♩♩♩♩♩♩♩♩ can be grouped into

♩♩♩♩♩ ♩♩♩♩♩ ♩♩♩♩♩ ♩♩ from which we can see what

the next note will be

♩♩♩♩♩ ♩♩♩♩♩ ♩♩♩♩♩ ♩♩♩

Chapter Twelve
Place Value

Fred watched the nurse stack up the pill boxes. After she got 9 of them, the next box she would chunk up to make a stack of ten.

$$9 \quad + \quad 1 \quad = \quad 10$$

The fun came when she had 99 boxes and got one more.

First she chunked the 9 boxes and the 1 box to make a stack of 10.

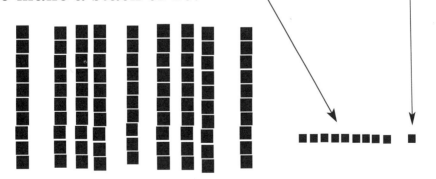

became

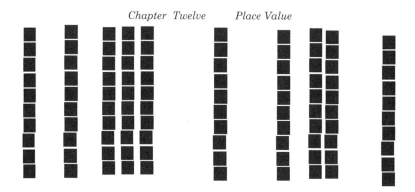

Then she chunked the 10 stacks into a square.

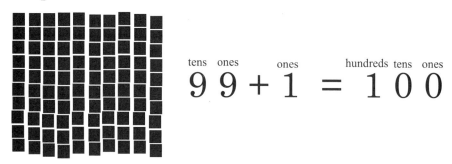

tens ones   ones   hundreds tens ones

$$9\ 9 + 1 = 1\ 0\ 0$$

When the nurse was finally done, she had three hundred twenty-four boxes.

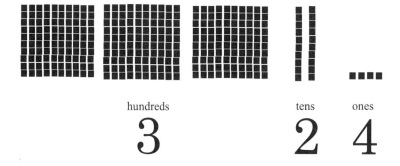

hundreds   tens ones

3   2 4

Fred thought about the math classes he would be teaching today. Having the nurse come into each of his classes and stack pill boxes would be the perfect way to teach place value.

There are ten digits in our decimal system:*
0, 1, 2, 3, 4, 5, 6, 7, 8, and 9.

Where the digits sit makes a difference. So
23 is different than 32. Fred would have the
nurse stack up boxes to show the difference.

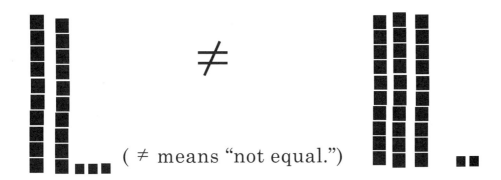

(≠ means "not equal.")

Then Fred would have her stack up 999
boxes. That would be 9 hundreds, 9 tens, and 9
ones. Then he would dramatically add one more
box. The 9 ones plus one more would make a stack of ten. The ten stacks of
ten would then turn into a square of a hundred boxes. Then she would have
ten hundreds and would turn that into a cube with a thousand boxes in it.

$$999 + 1 = \underset{\text{thousands}}{1}\ \underset{\text{hundreds}}{0}\ \underset{\text{tens}}{0}\ \underset{\text{ones}}{0}$$

---

* Our system with ten digits is called the decimal system. The oldest place value
system was the sexagesimal system invented in the Babylonian Empire (around 2000
B.C.). They had 60 different digits. Actually, they only had 59 digits since they
didn't have a zero. They just used a space for a zero. So if they wanted to write 705,
they would write 7 5. If they wanted to write 7005, they would write 7   5.

   Zeros are nice.

Then for the finale* Fred would have a truck deliver all the pill boxes in Kansas into the hallway outside of his classroom.

Then the nurse would spend several days stacking up the pill boxes. Every time she got ten of them, she would make a stack of ten. Every time she had ten stacks of ten, she would make a square of a hundred. And ten hundreds would turn into a thousand.

And then Fred could show his students what five million, three hundred sixty-seven thousand, nine hundred forty-eight boxes looked like.

millions	hundred thousands	ten thousands	thousands	hundreds	tens	ones
5,	3	6	7,	9	4	8

And there would be a big sign:

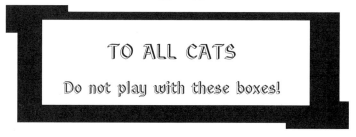

TO ALL CATS

Do not play with these boxes!

---

* fin-AL-ee   A finale is the last part of a performance.

Fred turned to the nurse who had just finished stacking up 324 boxes. He asked her what she thought about stacking up 5,367,948 boxes in the hallway outside of his classroom.

She laughed and left the room.

Your Turn to Play

1.   1   1   1
     + 9   + 99   + 9999999

2.   100
      − 1

3. Write five million in numerals.

4. Here is the set of animals or people who have laughed at Fred recently: {kitty, nurse}. What is the cardinality of that set?

5. Name the biggest ocean in the world.

6. Are you an obligate carnivore?

7. In question 6, what word is an adjective?

8. (This is a harder question.) What is the next one in this sequence:

. . . . ANSWERS . . . .

1.
$$
\begin{array}{r} 1 \\ +\ 9 \\ \hline 10 \end{array}
\qquad
\begin{array}{r} 1 \\ +\ 99 \\ \hline 100 \end{array}
\qquad
\begin{array}{r} 1 \\ +\ 9{,}999{,}999 \\ \hline 10{,}000{,}000 \end{array}
$$

2.
$$
\begin{array}{r} 100 \\ -\ 1 \\ \hline 99 \end{array}
$$

3. Five million = 5,000,000

4. The cardinality of {kitty, nurse} is 2.

5. The Pacific Ocean is the biggest ocean in the world.

6. Humans are not obligate carnivores. They can eat and digest plants as well as meat. Have you ever had fried zucchini?

7. *Obligate* is an adjective. This was a hard question. I hope that you didn't just look at the question and then look at my answer. Learning how to make an effort is a very valuable skill to learn.

8. ❀✲❀✲✲❀✲✲✲❀✲✲✲✲ could be seen as:

❀✲   ❀✲✲   ❀✲✲✲   ❀✲✲✲✲   ❀✲✲✲✲✲

1   1   1   2   1   3   1   4   ☞

Chapter Thirteen
Jogging

When Fred walked out of the KITTENS hospital it was dawn— one of Fred's favorite times of the day. The flat land of Kansas stretched out before him. Teaching his Tuesday classes was still several hours away.

He felt happy. Instead of breaking out into a song that he made up,

he started running. Jogging was something he did on many mornings. It made him feel good to run in the cool air of the morning.

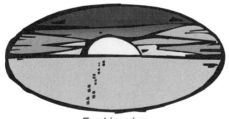

Fred jogging

Fred had been jogging on the KITTENS University campus for years. He had begun teaching at KITTENS when he was nine months old. (The whole story is in *Life of Fred: Calculus*.)

When he was about two years old, he had seen some of his students jogging. He didn't know why they were doing that and was curious. He turned to books to find the answers. Prof. Eldwood's *Running for Fun and Health*, 1855, told him a lot.

So at the age of two, Fred began jogging around the campus.

At first, women would stop him and ask, "Where are you going little boy? Have you lost your mommy?" They had never seen a two-year-old boy out jogging for fun and health.

Then they would realize that this was Fred, and that he was their teacher in an algebra or a geometry class.

After a while, everyone on campus became used to seeing this little kid out jogging in the morning.

Today, Fred was going to limit his jog to an hour so that he would have plenty of time to prepare for teaching his classes.

In his head he practiced his addition tables. On a previous jog he had done all the numbers that add to 7:

$$
\begin{array}{ccccc}
1 & 2 & 3 & 4 & 5 \\
+\,6 & +\,5 & +\,4 & +\,3 & +\,2 \\
\hline
7 & 7 & 7 & 7 & 7
\end{array}
$$

And the numbers that add to 9:

$$
\begin{array}{ccccc}
2 & 3 & 4 & 5 & 6 \\
+\ 7 & +\ 6 & +\ 5 & +\ 4 & +\ 3 \\
\hline
9 & 9 & 9 & 9 & 9
\end{array}
$$

Today, he did those that add to 13:

$$
\begin{array}{ccccc}
4 & 5 & 6 & 7 & 8 \\
+9 & +8 & +7 & +6 & +5 \\
\hline
13 & 13 & 13 & 13 & 13
\end{array}
$$

Time Out!
Morse code

Back in the 1950s when I, your author, was a Boy Scout, we were required to learn the Morse code in order to become a First Class Scout.

We had to memorize the 26 letters:

A = ●—
B = —●●●
C = —●—●
. . .
Y = —●——
Z = ——●●

They no longer require that to become a First Class Scout. The world has changed (cell phones, etc.) and few people need Morse code today.

In contrast, learning your basic addition facts remains very important in today's world.

If you have a nickel (5¢) and 8 pennies, you will look like an idiot if you get out your calculator for

$$\begin{array}{r} 5 \\ + 8 \\ \hline 13 \end{array}$$

The goal is to instantly know the addition tables. Memorize! They are really much easier than the Morse code.

Here are the add-to-13 numbers. Study them. Say them aloud. Learn them <u>now</u>.

$$\begin{array}{r} 4 \\ + 9 \\ \hline 13 \end{array} \qquad \begin{array}{r} 5 \\ + 8 \\ \hline 13 \end{array} \qquad \begin{array}{r} 6 \\ + 7 \\ \hline 13 \end{array} \qquad \begin{array}{r} 7 \\ + 6 \\ \hline 13 \end{array} \qquad \begin{array}{r} 8 \\ + 5 \\ \hline 13 \end{array}$$

Please don't turn the page until you have these memorized. Please.

Remember, on the Your Turn to Plays you are to write your answers down before you turn the page and look at my answers.

Your Turn to Play

1. Name an ocean that is *not* the largest ocean in the world.

2. Add six apples plus seven apples.

3. Add four eggs plus five eggs.

4. The volume of the Pacific Ocean is approximately one hundred seventy million cubic miles. Write that number as a numeral.

5. Addition is commutative. If you add 5 and 8 you get the same answer as adding 8 and 5.

Draw some stars to show that 2 + 3 is equal to 3 + 2.

6. This square contains 100 boxes.

This stack contains 10 boxes.

All together, how many boxes are drawn below?

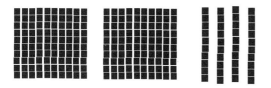

. . . . ANSWERS . . . .

1. There are four major oceans in the world. The Pacific Ocean is the largest. The other three are

the Atlantic Ocean

the Indian Ocean

and the Arctic Ocean

2. Six apples plus seven apples are 13 apples.
3. Four eggs plus five eggs are 9 eggs.
4. One hundred seventy million = 170,000,000.
5. ★ ★ + ★ ★ ★ = ★ ★ ★ + ★ ★

    2   +   3   3   +   2

    hundreds   tens   ones
6.   2   4   5

A Row of Practice

Cover the gray answers with a blank sheet of paper. Write your answers on your paper.

Then after you have done the whole row, check your answers.

6	9	5	4	5	8	8	15
+ 7	+ 4	+ 4	+ 3	+ 2	+ 5	+ 1	+ 1
13	13	9	7	7	13	9	16

Chapter Fourteen
Cents

Fred chanted as he jogged. Five and eight are thirteen. Five and eight are thirteen. The sun felt warm on his face. The air was pleasantly cool.

He ran along the pathways through the campus. KITTENS University was founded in 1929. Shortly after it was founded, the gardener planted many trees along the pathways.

After a half century, they had grown tall and beautiful.

A century is 100 years.

A half century is 50 years.

A dollar is 100 cents.

A half dollar is 50 cents.

A centenarian is a person who has lived 100 years.

A centurion is a commander of 100 men in the Roman army.

A percent is one part out of a 100.

Fred loved the scent of the pine trees[*] that had been planted along the pathways.

He started to giggle as he ran. He thought of *cent,* and then of *scent,* and then of *sent.*

He tried to make up a sentence that had all three of those words in it. The best he could do was: *It didn't cost the pine tree a cent when it sent a scent into the air.*

Cent, sent, and *scent* are homonyms. They have the same sound (pronunciation) but different meanings.[**] *To, too,* and *two* are homonyms.

Some people like to collect homonyms. Whenever they find them, they write them down. Sometimes they are *allowed* to read them *aloud.*

The best that Fred ever found was four words that were homonyms. It occurred to him when he saw an ad for an 18-karat gold ring. Eighteen karats meant that 18 parts out of every 24 in the ring were gold. If a ring were 22 karats,

---

[*] Not all pine trees can survive Kansas winters. The Swiss Stone Pine is very hardy. It won't be harmed if the temperature were 35 degrees below zero. (−35°)

[**] English is much harder than math. It would be really simple if homonyms (HOM-eh-nims) were just words that were spelled differently and sounded alike. (*Ann* and *an*; *ate* and *eight*; *Barry, berry,* and *bury.*)

Or even more complicated. Homonyms can be words that are spelled alike and are pronounced alike, but have different meanings. (*fleet* of cars and *fleet* meaning speedy.)

that would mean that 22 parts out of every 24 in the ring were gold.

Twenty-four karats is pure gold.

Later, when we work with fractions, we can say that an 18-karat ring is $\frac{18}{24}$ gold.

In that same ad, Fred saw a diamond that was 10 carats. A carat is a weight. (A karat was a fraction. One karat = 1/24 pure gold.)

You weigh diamonds in carats. Five carats is about the weight of a raisin.

The third homonym was caret. This is a caret: ^. Proofreaders use carets to insert things that were left out.

If I wrote: `Joe the pizza,`

a proofreader might write `Joe` *ate* `the pizza.`

And, of course, the fourth homonym is

carrot.

karat	one twenty-fourth pure gold
carat	one-fifth of a gram
caret	insertion mark
carrot	to be eaten

Four* homonyms—karat, carat, caret, carrot, Fred thought to himself. *That has got to be a world's record.*

Fred had jogged for almost an hour. He had gone six miles.

Six miles is a length.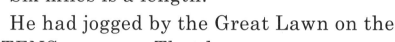

He had jogged by the Great Lawn on the KITTENS campus. That lawn had an area of about 3,688 square feet.

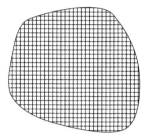

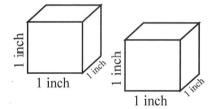

He stopped at the water fountain and drank two cubic inches of water. (That is just a little over an ounce of water.**)

---

*   Four = 4.

Fore = in front as in "come to the fore."

For = preposition as in "for my sake."

Prepositional phrases begin with prepositions. Here is a sentence with too many prepositional phrases: <u>In the spring</u>, <u>of the three things</u> I love doing, heading <u>toward the pizza restaurant</u> that is <u>by the bank</u> <u>across the street</u> <u>from my house</u> is, <u>in my opinion</u>, the most exciting activity <u>under the sun</u>.

Here are some prepositions: aboard, about, above, across, after, against, along, amid, among, anti, around, as, at, before, behind, below, beneath, beside, besides, between, beyond, but, by, concerning, considering, despite, down, during, ere, except, excepting, excluding, following, for, from, in, inside, into, like, minus, near, of, off, on, onto, opposite, outside, over, past, per, plus, regarding, round, save, since, than, through, to, toward, towards, under, underneath, unlike, until, up, upon, versus, via, with, within, without.

** One ounce = 1.805 cubic inches

Fred's jogging had taken him through:

Length   six miles

Area   3,688 square feet

Volume   two cubic inches.

In geometry, these are associated with

Segment   Square   Cube

Length   **Area**   **Volume**

Your Turn to Play

1. How are each of these measured? (Length, area, or volume?)

A) a piece of string

B) gasoline

C) how far it is to the North Pole

D) the size of Kansas

2. From the list of prepositions in the footnote on the previous page, choose five of them and write five prepositional phrases. (For example, if I chose *aboard,* I might write *aboard the train.*)

3. Add 3 cubic inches and 6 cubic inches.

Add 8 square yards and 5 square yards.

Add 7 miles and 6 miles.

......**ANSWERS**.......

1. A) A piece of string might be 6 inches. It is a length.

B) Gasoline is measured as a volume (in gallons or liters).

C) How far it is to the North Pole is a length (in miles or kilometers).

D) The size of Kansas is an area (82,282 square miles).

2. Your answers will be different than mine. Did you notice that my question had five prepositional phrases in it? <u>From the list</u> <u>of prepositions</u> <u>in the footnote</u> <u>on the previous page</u>, choose five <u>of them</u> and write five prepositional phrases.

3.   3 cubic inches plus 6 cubic inches equals 9 cubic inches.

    8 square yards plus 5 square yards equals 13 square yards.

    7 miles plus 6 miles equals 13 miles.

Some readers want to know what comes *before*

       Segment   Square   Cube

Many adults know the answer to that question:

Point   Segment   Square   Cube

Some readers want to know what comes *after* point, segment, square, and cube. The answer is a tesseract. (Few adults know that.) It is pictured on the cover of *Life of Fred: Geometry* and explained in detail in Chapter 12½ of that book.

Chapter Fifteen
To the Dictionary

Fred thought about taking his geometry class out for a little jog around the Great Lawn today. Then they could have a little drink at the water fountain. It would be the perfect way to teach them about length, area, and volume.

He thought that area would be the hardest of the three concepts to teach. Everyone knew how far they ran (length), and everyone knew what a pint of ice cream was (volume).

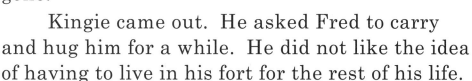

When he got back to his office from his morning jog, Fred told Kingie that he could come out of his fort now. The kitty was gone.

Kingie came out. He asked Fred to carry and hug him for a while. He did not like the idea of having to live in his fort for the rest of his life.

Fred picked Kingie up and gave him a big hug. Together, they pulled Fred's big dictionary off the shelf and took it to his desk.

Fred set Kingie on his desk. He got three phone books and put them on his chair. When Fred sat on the three phone books, he was tall enough to work at his desk.

Fred wanted to look up the word *area* in his dictionary. That might help him explain that idea to his geometry class. He read:

area (pronounced AIR–ee–eh) An extent of space.

That did not help at all. Fred was about to shut the dictionary when Kingie shouted, "Look at the word right above **area**!"

are (pronounced AIR) 100 square meters.

"Weird," Fred exclaimed. "*Are* is a measure of area. I bet that very few of my students know that."

Fred was e'er (ever) on the search for homonyms, and ere* Fred could close the dictionary, he said, "Unless I err,** I think I'm heir to a new world's record in homonyms." He took a big gulp of air.

Six!   air, are, e'er, ere, err, and heir.

---

* *Ere* is a preposition. It means "before."

** *Err* means to make a mistake.

Fred told Kingie, "I can use an are, which is 100 square meters, to talk about the metric system in my classes. I am one yard tall."

------------------one yard --------------------

That's 36 inches. $36 = 12 + 12 + 12$.

When I talk about square yards in my classroom, it's easy. I just lie down on the floor and have the students draw a square.

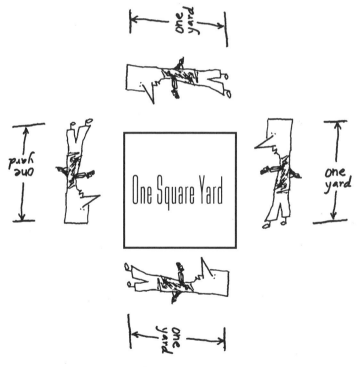

But Fred couldn't figure out how to show a square meter in his classroom. A meter is about 39 inches, and Fred is only 36 inches. At the rate that Fred has been growing, it may take years for him to be a meter tall.

Kingie had a suggestion: "Why don't you just let me sit on top of your head. You are 36 inches and I am 6 inches."

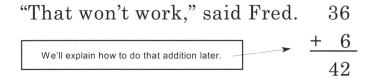

"That won't work," said Fred.   36

| We'll explain how to do that addition later. |

$$\begin{array}{r} 36 \\ +\ 6 \\ \hline 42 \end{array}$$

"I need to be 39 inches tall in order to be a meter tall."

$$\begin{array}{r} 36 \quad \text{Fred's height} \\ +\ 3 \quad\quad\quad\quad \\ \hline 39 \quad \text{one meter} \end{array}$$

Fred needed to add three inches to his height.

Kingie had all kinds of suggestions, but Fred didn't like any of them.

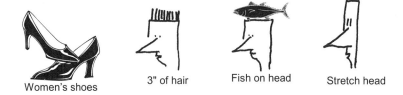

Women's shoes   3" of hair   Fish on head   Stretch head

Fred's idea wasn't much better:

Wear a 3" pizza

Kingie had a different thought: "Why do you want to teach about the metric system? What good is a meter?"

"Some people think that the metric system is easier," Fred explained.

"Ha!" shouted Kingie. "Nothing could be easier than yards. 1 yard = 3 feet. 1 foot = 12 inches. 1 mile = 5,280 feet. That's easy."

Fred smiled. "In the metric system, 1 meter = 100 centimeters. 1 kilometer = 1,000 meters."

Your Turn to Play

1. It is easy to see that if 1 kilometer = 1,000 meters, then 2 kilometers = 2,000 meters,

   3 kilometers = 3,000 meters, and
   8 kilometers = 8,000 meters.

We know that 1 mile = 5,280 feet.

Question: Would you like to figure out how many feet are in 8 miles? □ Yes or □ No.

2. Area can be measured in square inches, square feet, square yards, or square miles.

   One square mile = 27,878,400 square feet.
   One square kilometer = 1,000,000 square meters.

Seven square kilometers is seven million square meters. Would you like to figure out how many square feet are in seven square miles? □ Yes or □ No.

·······ANSWERS·······

1. No.

If 1 mile equals 5,280 feet, then one way to figure out how many feet are in eight miles would be to add:

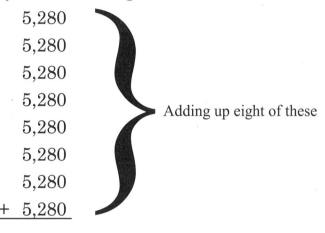

5,280
5,280
5,280
·5,280
5,280
5,280
5,280
+ 5,280

Adding up eight of these

2. No.

If 1 square mile equals 27,878,400 square feet, then one way to figure out how many square feet are in seven square miles would be to add:

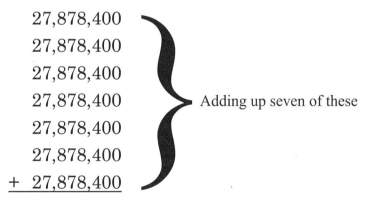

27,878,400
27,878,400
27,878,400
27,878,400
27,878,400
27,878,400
+ 27,878,400

Adding up seven of these

For fun, I did the work. Seven 27,878,400s added together equal 195,148,800. There are one hundred ninety-five million, one hundred forty-eight thousand, eight hundred square feet in seven square miles.

Chapter Sixteen
Measuring

Kingie didn't like the metric system. All of his life he had used the Imperial system.* He couldn't see anything wrong with

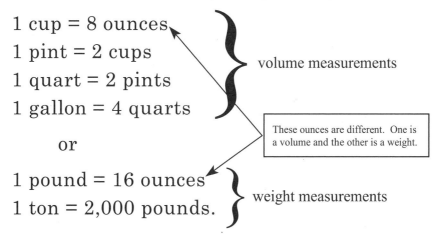

1 cup = 8 ounces
1 pint = 2 cups
1 quart = 2 pints
1 gallon = 4 quarts
} volume measurements

These ounces are different. One is a volume and the other is a weight.

or

1 pound = 16 ounces
1 ton = 2,000 pounds.
} weight measurements

Fred pointed out to Kingie that in the metric system, volume is much easier. One liter = 1,000 milliliters. Weight is also much easier. One kilogram = 1,000 grams.

Kingie wouldn't accept any of that. He was in a **BAD MOOD** because his whole morning had been bad. He just wanted to argue. Before today, he had been able to run around Fred's office and do his painting undisturbed. When Fred brought

---

* The Imperial system uses inches, feet, yards, miles, ounces, pounds, tons, quarts, etc.

home that obligate carnivore, Kingie feared for his life. He had to retreat to his tiny fort in the corner of his room.

Kingie told Fred, "If that stupid metric system is so good, why doesn't everybody use it? Everyone I know uses the Imperial system of feet and pounds and quarts."

"How many people do you know?" Fred asked. The only people that Kingie had ever met were Fred, Alexander, Betty, Joe, and Darlene.

Fred showed Kingie two lists:

Countries in the World
that Primarily Use Metric

Afghanistan, Albania, Algeria, Andorra, Angola, Antigua and Barbuda, Argentina, Armenia, Australia, Austria, Azerbaijan, The Bahamas, Bahrain, Bangladesh, Barbados, Belarus, Belgium, Belize, Benin, Bhutan, Bolivia, Bosnia and Herzegovina, Botswana, Brazil, Brunei, Bulgaria, Burkina Faso, Burundi, Cambodia, Cameroon, Canada, Cape Verde, Central African Republic, Chad, Chile, China, Colombia, Comoros, Costa Rica, Cote d'Ivoire, Croatia, Cuba, Cyprus, Czech Republic, Denmark, Djibouti, Dominica, Dominican Republic, East Timor, Ecuador, Egypt, El Salvador, Equatorial Guinea, Eritrea, Estonia, Ethiopia, Fiji, Finland, France, Gabon, The Gambia, Georgia, Germany, Ghana, Greece, Grenada, Guatemala, Guinea, Guinea-Bissau, Guyana, Haiti, Honduras, Hungary, Iceland, India, Indonesia, Iran, Iraq, Ireland, Israel, Italy, Jamaica, Japan, Jordan, Kazakhstan, Kenya, Kiribati, Korea, North, Korea, South, Kosovo, Kuwait, Kyrgyzstan, Laos, Latvia, Lebanon, Lesotho, Libya, Liechtenstein, Lithuania, Luxembourg, Macedonia, Madagascar, Malawi, Malaysia, Maldives, Mali, Malta, Marshall Islands, Mauritania, Mauritius, Mexico, Micronesia, Federated States of Moldova, Monaco, Mongolia, Montenegro, Morocco, Mozambique, Namibia, Nauru, Nepal, Netherlands, New Zealand, Nicaragua, Niger, Nigeria, Norway, Oman, Pakistan, Palau, Panama, Papua New Guinea, Paraguay, Peru, Philippines, Poland, Portugal, Qatar, Romania, Russia, Rwanda, Saint Kitts and Nevis, Saint Lucia, Saint Vincent and the Grenadines, Samoa, San Marino, Sao Tome and Principe, Saudi Arabia, Senegal, Serbia, Seychelles, Sierra Leone, Singapore, Slovakia, Slovenia, Solomon Islands, Somalia, South Africa, Spain, Sri Lanka, Sudan, Suriname, Swaziland, Sweden, Switzerland, Syria, Taiwan, Tajikistan, Tanzania, Thailand, Togo, Tonga, Trinidad and Tobago, Tunisia, Turkey, Turkmenistan, Tuvalu, Uganda, Ukraine, United Arab Emirates, United Kingdom, Uruguay, Uzbekistan, Vanuatu, Vatican City, Venezuela, Vietnam, Yemen, Zambia, and Zimbabwe.

All the Countries
that Aren't Primarily Metric

Liberia, Myanmar, and the U.S.A.

Kingie didn't like arguing with Fred. Fred knew too much. Kingie headed back into his fort and shut the door.

He was going to relax and do some oil painting. He was good at that. In fact, he was much better at art than Fred.

He set up his easel and got out his tubes of oil paint. He took out his favorite Yellow Ochre 150 mL* tube and squeezed out a dab of paint onto his palette. Then he squeezed out some Venetian Red from a 120 mL tube. He didn't like black oil paint so he only had a 12 mL tube of Ivory Black.

Kingie was happy doing his painting, even though his oil paint tubes were sold in metric units.

Fred needed to get ready to teach his Tuesday classes.

---

* mL means milliliter. 1000 mL = 1 liter. It's metric, but Kingie didn't realize that. Sometimes mL is written as ml.

    A liter is a little bigger than a quart—just like a meter is a little bigger than a yard.

Fred hopped on top of the three phone books on his chair and looked at his desk.

He looked at his morning schedule:

```
8-9       Arithmetic
9-10      Beginning Algebra
10-11     Advanced Algebra
11-noon   Geometry
```

He took some string and divided the top of his desk into four equal areas.

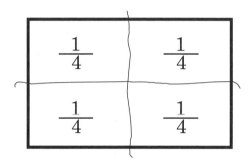

He would use one-fourth of his desk for each of the four subjects he was going to teach in the morning. He put a blank sheet of paper in each quarter of the desk.

Your Turn to Play

Here is what Fred wrote on
his lecture notes for his classes:

Arithmetic

1. Show that
   5 + 8 = 13 by
   drawing five
   horses and eight
   horses.

2. Show a set with
   cardinality equal
   to five.

On your sheet of paper
write out the answers
to his questions.

Algebra

3. 5x + 8x = ?

4. 9y + 4y = ?

5. 6abc + 7abc = ?

6. What value of
   x makes this true?
   x + 5 = 13

Geometry

7. Draw a segment,
   a square, and
   a cube.

8. Draw a triangle
   where all three
   sides have the
   same length.

· · · · · · · **ANSWERS** · · · · · · ·

1. Your horses may look different than Fred's.

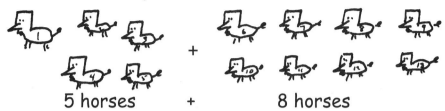

       5 horses   +   8 horses

2. Sets are written with braces.

      These are braces   {   }.

      These are parentheses (   ).

      These are brackets   [   ].

Here are some sets with cardinality equal to five.

Your answer may be different than these examples.

$\{ \blacksquare, \triangle, \copyright, \boxtimes, \rightarrowtail \}$ $\{1, 2, 7, 8, 34397\}$ $\{\alpha, \beta, \gamma, \delta, \varepsilon\}^*$

3. $5x + 8x = 13x$ (just like five apples and eight apples are thirteen apples.)

4. $9y + 4y = 13y$

5. $6abc + 7abc = 13abc$

6. If $x = 8$, then $x + 5 = 13$ is true.

7.

    ——————

    Segment

            Square   Cube

8. small drawing $\triangle$ and large drawing

---

* α (alpha), β (beta), γ (gamma), δ (delta), and ε (epsilon) are the first five letters of the Greek alphabet. When you get to Trig and Calculus, which are the two courses that come right after   Arithmetic,

          Pre-algebra,

            Beginning Algebra,

              Advanced Algebra, and

                Geometry, you will start to use a lot of Greek letters.

Chapter Seventeen
Into Rectangles

Fred did not stop teaching at noon. From noon to 1 p.m. he taught Trig.* From 1 p.m. to 2 p.m. he taught Calculus.

He got out some more string and divided the top of his desk into six equal areas.

Arithmetic	Beginning Algebra	Advanced Algebra
Geometry	Trig	Calculus

That looked very neat.

If he had only five courses, he couldn't make them into a rectangle.

The only thing he could do with five courses is put them into a line: ● ● ● ● ●.

Two courses could only go in a line: ●●.

Three could only go in a line: ●●●.

Four could go in a rectangle: ●●
●●

---

* Trig is short for trigonometry. Trig deals with triangles and angles.

Six could go into a rectangle: ●●●
●●●

or they could go: ●●
●●   Two rows of 3
●●   or three rows of 2

Seven could only go in a line: ●●●●●●● .

Eight could go into a rectangle: ●●●●
●●●●

or ●●
●●   Two rows of 4
●●   or four rows of 2
●●

Fred looked at this and shouted, "Wow!"

Kingie opened his fort door and looked out at Fred. "Are you okay?" he asked. He was worried that Fred had hurt himself. Kingie was in a better mood now. Doing some oil painting had made him feel better.

Fred was gleeful, jubilant, ecstatic, rapturous. In short, he was pretty happy. He had discovered a neat way to play with numbers.

This would be perfect for his arithmetic class. He had just invented a new game for his students to play.

He was going to call his new game Rectangulable Numbers. He would give a number to his students, and they would figure out whether it could be put into a rectangle.

There was only one problem. Fred had made up the word *rectangulable,* but it was almost impossible to pronounce.

If he said *rectangulable* several times he would get his tang tongueled—his tongue tangled.

He changed the name of his game to Boxable Numbers. There is no such word as *boxable*, but at least it could be pronounced.

What numbers could be put into a box (into a rectangle) and what numbers could only go in a line?

There are three kinds of numbers:

The number 1 ● which can't be made into a line or a box.	The boxable numbers: 4 ●● ●● 6 ●●● ●●● 8 ●●●● ●●●● 10 ●●●●● ●●●●●	The numbers that can only go in a line: 2 ●● 3 ●●● 5 ●●●●● 7 ●●●●●●●

Time out!
What Mathematicians Do

In the early years of your life, you learn about the different things that adults do. That helps you decide what you want to do in the later years of your life.

Some jobs are easy to understand. A maid cleans. A gardener gardens. Painters paint.

What do mathematicians do? Have you ever seen a mathematician at work? Almost everyone has seen someone
* mopping a floor,
    * digging a hole, or
       * painting a building.
You have seen
          * dentists drilling,
      * teachers teaching, and
* letter carriers carrying letters.

But not one adult in a hundred has ever seen what mathematicians really do.

The secret is . . . they play.

Mathematicians explore and discover. They explore the world of numbers and shapes. They discover new things that no one else has ever known.

Your Turn to Play

1. Fred was *exploring* the world of boxable numbers. Except for 1 and 2, he noticed that:

★ all the even numbers (4, 6, 8, 10, . . .) were boxable

4 ●●
6 ●●●
   ●●●
8 ●●●●
   ●●●●
10 ●●●●●
    ●●●●●

★ all the odd numbers (3, 5, 7, . . .) could only go in a straight line.

3 ●●●
5 ●●●●●
7 ●●●●●●●

Fred was trying to *discover* the truth. But he was in for a surprise.

Show that 9 (an odd number) is boxable. In other words, show that it can be put into a rectangle of dots.

2. Show that 15 (an odd number) is also boxable.

3. What about even numbers? Is every even number that is larger than 2 a boxable number? What is your guess?

·······ANSWERS·······

1. 9 is boxable.

2. 15 is boxable. You can make two different rectangles:

     Three rows of 5
or five rows of 3

3. If you guessed that every even number greater than two is boxable, you were right.

4   ●●
6   ●●●
    ●●●
8   ●●●●
    ●●●●
10 ●●●●●
    ●●●●●
12 ●●●●●●
    ●●●●●●
14 ●●●●●●●
    ●●●●●●●
16 ●●●●●●●●
    ●●●●●●●●
18 ●●●●●●●●●
    ●●●●●●●●●
20 ●●●●●●●●●●
    ●●●●●●●●●●
22 ●●●●●●●●●●●
    ●●●●●●●●●●●

etc.   even numbers = {2, 4, 6, 8, . . .}

odd numbers = {1, 3, 5, 7, . . .}

Chapter Eighteen
Getting Dressed

Fred was excited. It wasn't as easy as *All the even numbers (larger than 2) were boxable, and all the odd numbers (larger than 2) were not boxable.*

You could box some of the odd numbers. Math is full of unexpected surprises. It is only dull if it is poorly taught.

Fred had the fun of finding a new way of dividing up the natural numbers {1, 2, 3, 4, . . .}. He put them into three different categories.

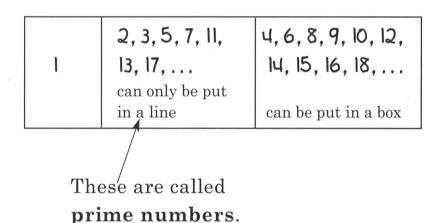

1	2, 3, 5, 7, 11, 13, 17, . . . can only be put in a line	4, 6, 8, 9, 10, 12, 14, 15, 16, 18, . . . can be put in a box

These are called
prime numbers.

Some mathematicians fall in love with prime numbers and play with them all the time. They have discovered many things about the prime numbers.

For example, prime numbers get rarer and rarer as you go up into the natural numbers.

In the first hundred natural numbers, the set of primes is {2, 3, 5, 7, 11, 13, 17, 19, 23, 29, 31, 37, 41, 43, 47, 53, 59, 61, 67, 71, 73, 79, 83, 89, 97}. There are **25 primes** in this set.

In the hundred natural numbers from 2901 to 3000, there are only **11 primes**: {2903, 2909, 2917, 2927, 2939, 2953, 2957, 2963, 2969, 2971, 2999}.

In the hundred natural numbers from 104,401 to 104,500, there are only **6 primes**: {104417, 104459, 104471, 104473, 104479, 104491}.

One mathematician found a million natural numbers in a row (consecutive natural numbers) where not one of them is prime.*

---

* (Please do not read this footnote until you have had algebra.)
In later math we define 6! to mean 6×5×4×3×2×1. (It's called six factorial.)
Here is a list of one million consecutive non-prime numbers:
1,000,002! + 2, 1,000,002! + 3, 1,000,002! + 4, . . . , 1,000,002! + 1,000,001.
　　　　Note, for example, that 1,000,002! + 683 is evenly divisible by 683 and therefore is not prime.

Fred looked at the clock. It was ten minutes to eight. His arithmetic class starts at eight.

7:50 a.m.

He didn't want to be late.

Fred liked to always wear a bow tie when he taught. He thought that that made him look older.

He put one on, gathered up his lecture notes, and was about to head out the door when Kingie said, "Wait!"

Kingie pointed to what Fred was wearing. He was still in his pajamas.

Fred had gone back to his sleeping bag at a quarter to three this morning.

Since then, he had been awoken by his kitty.

He had been to the doctor's.

He had jogged for an hour around KITTENS campus.

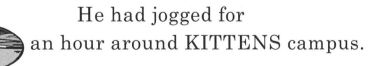

But Fred had never changed out of his pajamas.

Fred put on a shirt and then tried to take off his pajama top. That didn't work.

You take off your pajama top before you put on your shirt. Those two things are not commutative.

Fred's nose was much better. If he had been really old, like 18 years old, it would have taken longer to heal.

He gave Kingie a hug and
≫headed out the door,
  ≫down the hallway past the 9 vending
    machines (5 on one side and 4 on the other),
     ≫down two flights of stairs, and
      ≫out into the morning air.

There were zillions of students headed off to class.

Many of them were heading to the Archimedes building to hear Fred teach.

Fred had been thinking of the set of natural numbers: {1, 2, 3, 4, . . . }.

He thought of the set of all those students:

Your Turn to Play

1. Fred could divide the natural numbers into two sets: the odd numbers {1, 3, 5, 7, . . .} and the even numbers {2, 4, 6, 8, . . . }.

He could divide the set of all those students into two sets: those born in Kansas and those who weren't born in Kansas.

Think of three other ways to divide that set of students into two sets.

2. Fred could divide the natural numbers into three sets: {1}, the prime numbers {2, 3, 5, 7, 11, . . . } and the numbers that could be put in a box {4, 6, 8, 9, . . . }.

Divide the set of students into three sets.

3. (hard questions)

A) divide the set of students into 7 sets

B) into 12 sets

C) into 26 sets

·······ANSWERS·······

1. Your answers may be different than mine.

Ways to divide the set of students into two sets:

☞ Male and female students.

☞ Those born in California and those who weren't born in California.

☞ Those who weigh less than 100 pounds and those who don't.

☞ Those who are taking Fred's class at 8 o'clock today and those who aren't.

☞ Those who are wearing a hat right now and those who aren't.

☞ Those who are carrying five books right now and those who aren't.

☞ Those who had pizza for breakfast today and those who didn't.

2. Ways to divide the set of students into three sets:

☞ Those born in Kansas; those born in Nebraska; and the rest.

☞ Those whose favorite color is blue; those whose favorite color is red; and the rest.

☞ Those who have four sisters; those who have five sisters; and the rest.

3. A) Divide into seven sets by the day of the week that they were born on.

B) Divide into 12 sets by which month their mother was born in.

C) Divide into 26 sets by the first letter in their last name.

   Or into 26 sets: Those who watched no televison programs in the last month into the first set. Those who watched one TV program in the last month into the second set. . . . Those who watched 24 TV programs in the last month into the twenty-fifth set. Those who watched 25 or more programs in the last month into the twenty-sixth set.

Chapter Nineteen
On the Way to Class

Fred often took different paths each day as he headed off to teach in the Archimedes building.

At first, he thought of going back and seeing all the stone statues that he had seen yesterday. They were near the Great Woods.

He thought of . . .

standing on the
head of the
Cowardly Lion

saying hello
to Dorothy

feeling the straw
of the Scarecrow

patting Dorothy's
dog on the head

But he had only about three minutes before his eight o'clock class, so he headed straight through the crowd of students.

He giggled as he walked. He thought of writing a children's book entitled:

Where's Fredo?

The only problem is that even if you looked for hours, you would never be able to see Fred.

Fred is three feet tall, and almost all of the students are between five and six feet tall.

Three feet is less than five feet. In symbols, *three is less than five* is written 3 < 5.

The stone statue of Dorothy is 12 feet tall. Fred is much shorter than Dorothy. 3 < 12.

In fact, 3 < 🐱

Fred couldn't think of anyone who was shorter than he was. Fred was wrong.*

Your Turn to Play

1. This is the set of natural numbers: {1, 2, 3, 4, . . .}. Suppose x is a natural number and x < 2. What would x equal?

2. Suppose y is a natural number, y is a prime, and y < 6. What different values could y have?

3. Suppose that z is a natural number and z < 8. *How many* different values could z have?

4. What time does this clock say?

5. A century is how many years?
A dollar is how many cents?
A centenarian is a person who has lived how many years?

6. Eight pencils plus five pencils = ?

7. Write four thousand in numerals.

......ANSWERS.......

1. x = 1. There is only one natural number that is less than 2.

2. The set of prime natural numbers less than six is {2, 3, 5}. So y could equal 2, 3 or 5.

3. Here is the set of natural numbers less than 8: {1, 2, 3, 4, 5, 6, 7}. There are 7 members of that set.

4.

It is 2:50 (or ten minutes to three).

5. A century is 100 years.

    A dollar is 100 cents.

    A centenarian is a person who has lived 100 years.

6. Eight pencils plus five pencils is 13 pencils.

7. 4,000

thousands   hundreds   tens   ones

4,0 0 0

Index

If you would like to
learn more about
books written about
Fred . . .

FredGauss.com

Gauss is Fred's last name.

It rhymes with house.